USA TODAY **TEEN WISE GUIDES**

A GANNETT COMPANY

TIME, MONEY, AND RELATIONSHIPS

JOB
SMARTS

How to Find Work or Start a Business, Manage Earnings, and More

SANDY DONOVAN

T F
C B

TWENTY-FIRST CENTURY BOOKS / MINNEAPOLIS

Twenty-First Century Books
A division of Lerner Publishing Group, Inc.
241 First Avenue North
Minneapolis, MN 55401 U.S.A.

Website address: www.lernerbooks.com

Library of Congress Cataloging-in-Publication Data

Donovan, Sandra, 1967–
    Job smarts : how to find work or start a business, manage earnings, and more / by Sandra Donovan.
        p. cm. — (USA TODAY teen wise guides: time, money, and relationships)
    Includes bibliographical references and index.
    ISBN 978–0–7613–7015–4 (lib. bdg. : alk. paper)
    1. Job hunting—Juvenile literature. 2. Vocational guidance—Juvenile literature. I. Title.
HF5382.7.D66 2012
650.14—dc23   2011021545

CONTENTS

If you don't have enough money to download the music your friends are able to, maybe it's time to get a job.

INTRODUCTION

I NEED Money!

School's out for the day, and your friends are getting together to check out the new music they bought this week. How come it seems as if everyone but you has the money to download music?

Then comes Saturday night, and everyone's going to see that new movie and then grab something to eat afterward. Once again, you don't have the cash to join in.

Earning money at a job can help you pay for the new clothes you yearn for.

Do you have a case of the money blues? You know—always feeling as if you're too poor to do what your friends are doing? Let's face it: you need more cash. So what exactly are your options? Your parents give you an allowance, but they have made it clear that they aren't going to shell out any extra. And even though your older brother seems as if he has money to burn, he sure isn't going to share with you.

What to do? It might be time to pick yourself up, hit the streets, and find a job. Wondering how on earth you're going to do that? You've picked up the right book!

1 ARE YOU READY
for a Job?

Do you think working at a coffee shop would be a good job for you? What about mowing lawns?

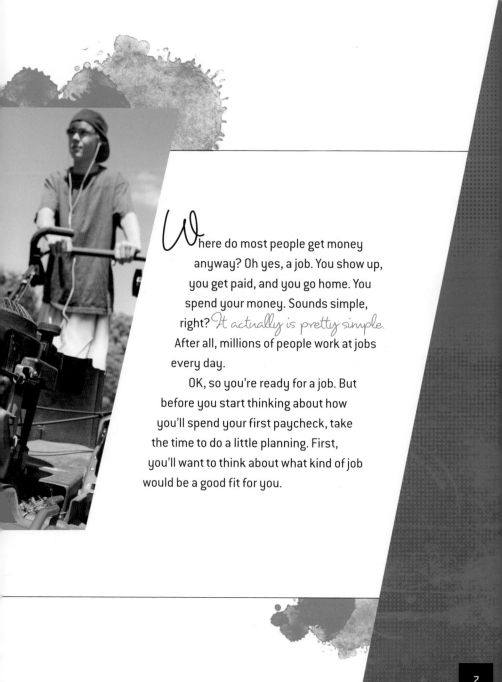

Where do most people get money anyway? Oh yes, a job. You show up, you get paid, and you go home. You spend your money. Sounds simple, right? It actually is pretty simple. After all, millions of people work at jobs every day.

OK, so you're ready for a job. But before you start thinking about how you'll spend your first paycheck, take the time to do a little planning. First, you'll want to think about what kind of job would be a good fit for you.

If you like to spend time outside, maybe yard work is a good job for you.

WHAT KIND OF JOB?

Think about spending a few hours each day staffing the espresso machine at a busy coffee shop. You'd have to act quickly, remember complicated orders, and interact with a lot of different people. You'd probably have to deal with complaints and even rude customers from time to time. Some people love this kind of fast-paced job. But for others, the stress might not be worth the paycheck.

If you like to work alone, you might enjoy a job shelving books at a library or answering phones for a small business. If you prefer the company of others, consider a job at an ice cream shop or a fast-food restaurant. But remember: if you get easily distracted by socializing, you may not want to put yourself in that kind of environment.

If the thought of being cooped up in a mall all day is enough to make you shiver, consider working outdoors at a swimming pool or at a kids' camp. Or you could do lawn work. If you like to be active, you might want to steer clear of jobs where you'd be sitting at a desk and answering phones or doing computer tasks.

HOW MUCH JOB IS ENOUGH?

Earning money can be important, but so are all your other commitments. School, extracurricular activities, homework, chores,

TOP JOBS FOR TEENS

Babysitter
Camp counselor
Coffee shop worker
Fast-food worker
Grocery bagger
Ice cream shop worker
Lifeguard
Nursing home assistant
Restaurant host
Restaurant table busser
Store assistant

LIFEGUARD

CEOs VALUE LESSONS FROM TEEN JOBS

By Del Jones

When he was 18, CEO [chief executive officer] David Haffner of manufacturer Leggett & Platt worked the graveyard [night] shift at a Hercules explosives plant in Missouri. Each night, Haffner and two others loaded 200,000 pounds [90,000 kilograms] of ammonium nitrate onto a railroad boxcar, one 50-pound [22 kg] bag at a time, hustling to finish early to squeeze in an hour of sleep at 6 A.M. before heading to classes at Missouri Southern State University. Haffner says he developed Popeye forearms making $3.86 an hour in 1971.

Today, Haffner, 55, runs a company with 24,000 employees. Long ago, his performance ceased to be measured by the perspiration on his brow. But hard labor was not foreign to him or to many CEOs as teens.

Jeff Rich, 47, the former CEO of Affiliated Computer, was a 13-year-old hay baler making $50 a day moving 2,000 bundles in 110° Fahrenheit [43°C] lofts. Tony White, 61, CEO of health care company Applera, says there may still be a footprint stain on his mother's bathtub from his job cleaning the oily soot from oil and coal furnaces in Asheville, North Carolina.

Did they learn important lessons from the drudgery that shapes their leadership style today? Almost all say yes. If nothing else, it taught them to finish college. "Demanding jobs motivated me to stay in school," says UPS CEO Scott Davis, 56, a former pear picker and lumber mill laborer.

and spending time with friends and family can easily overload anyone's calendar.

A job will make that calendar even more crowded. So how much should you work? Some teens work every day after school for a couple of hours. Others work only on weekends. Some work only during the summer or over school holidays.

Software Spectrum co-founder Judy Odom, 55, all but single-handedly ran a tuxedo rental shop for minimum wage as a 17-year-old in Fort Worth, Texas, where the owner showed up at day's end to empty the cash register. She remembers placing cold calls from newspaper engagement announcements and, on weekends, acting as chief troubleshooter as the store turned frenzied with last-minute needs. "I learned so much about business from that job, both do's and don'ts," Odom says.

Joe Herring, 52, CEO at Covance [a drug company], started out selling a $55.95, 2,500-page encyclopedia/homework manual. He was paid entirely on commission [based on how much he sold], and his daily goal was 60 calls, 20 to 30 demonstrations, and four or five sales. That usually required 14-hour days that often ended at 10 P.M. as the invited dinner guest of a customer. "My customers ranged from the blissfully happy to the divorced and depressed," Herring says. "Having 10 or 15 doors slammed in your face each day teaches about handling adversity and disappointment with a positive attitude. No matter how mean one family [was], the next could be a real gem," he says, adding that his success led to job offers at 10 other companies.

Outback Steakhouse founder Tim Gannon, 59, says he has yet to meet a successful person who didn't have a great story about starting at the ground floor. "Great success comes from overcoming adversity," Gannon says. "Without desire, you can't get to ambition."

—*June 6, 2008*

But even with a job, your first commitment as a teenager should always be school. You can earn money at a job and gain valuable work experience, but to really get ahead in the workplace, you'll need to complete your education. Keep this in mind as you consider your job options.

Think carefully about what you *won't* have time to do when you're

If you have a lot of time to watch TV, you might want to work more hours. Cut back on the time at your job if it cuts into your homework time.

working at a job. If your job will be cutting into only your TV watching or gaming hours, then it's probably worth your time. But if you won't have time for homework or after-school activities, you might look for a weekend job instead of an after-school job. Strive to find a balance between your school responsibilities, your extracurricular activities, your work, and your free time. Make a calendar of how you typically spend your time after school, on weekends, and on holidays. Try to find a time when you could work without taking away from other responsibilities.

Many teens are just too busy to hold a job during the school year. If that's the case for you, consider a summer job, such as lifeguarding or working as a camp counselor. By working full-time in summer, you might be able to save enough to have spending money during the school year.

DON'T TAKE IT LIGHTLY

Before you jump into a job, make sure you're really committed to the idea of working. Remember that once you accept a job, you need to show up on time and put in your best effort while you're there. At most jobs, you'll also have to get along with others—even others who might be very different from you.

Sounds pretty serious, right? *Holding a job is serious,* but it also offers you lots of benefits. The most obvious and important benefit is money. Earning money can help you meet your goals— from buying new clothes to buying a car to going to college. Earning your own money can also boost your financial independence, your self-confidence, and your money management skills. At most jobs, you'll gain valuable experience. You'll learn to work as part of a team and to work under pressure. These are skills you'll keep for the rest of your life.

USA TODAY Snapshots®

How workers found their latest jobs

Networking/word of mouth	61%
Newspaper ad	16%
Walk in/applied in person	9%
Newspaper Web site	5%
Internet job site	4%
Employment agency/recruiter	2%
Through school	1%

Percentages equal more than 100% due to rounding

Source: The Bernard Haldane Associates Internet Job Report conducted by Taylor Nelson Sofres Intersearch of 703 respondents

By Darryl Haralson and Sam Ward, USA TODAY, 2003

Surveys show that the best way to land a job is by word of mouth. If you're job hunting, tell your friends and family members. One of them might hear of a job that's a good fit for you.

2 LANDING a Job

Some employers put Help Wanted signs on their doors if they are hiring *(left)*. After you apply, you'll probably have a face-to-face interview *(right)*.

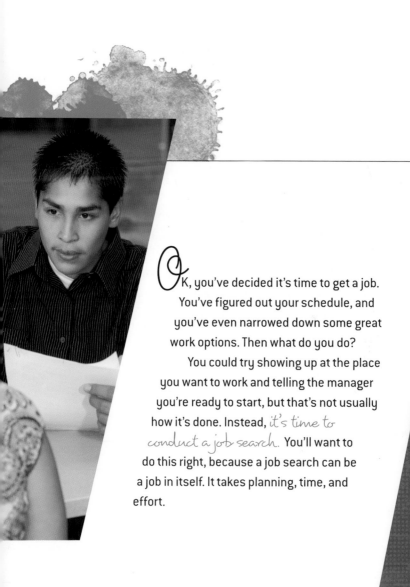

$\mathcal{O}$K, you've decided it's time to get a job. You've figured out your schedule, and you've even narrowed down some great work options. Then what do you do?

You could try showing up at the place you want to work and telling the manager you're ready to start, but that's not usually how it's done. Instead, *it's time to conduct a job search.* You'll want to do this right, because a job search can be a job in itself. It takes planning, time, and effort.

WHERE TO LOOK FOR A JOB

Where do you look first? Many employers advertise jobs on websites. You can search through the listings to see what qualifications an employer is looking for, how much a job pays, and how many hours are required. Some of the largest job websites are Monster and CareerBuilder. Snagajob lists only jobs that pay by the hour, and these are often good jobs for teens. Beware of job postings that sound too good to be true, though. For instance, jobs that offer hundreds of dollars a week to work from home are often scams.

Some employers post job openings on their own websites and even right at their businesses. Look for Help Wanted or Accepting Applications signs in the windows of stores and restaurants. Never underestimate the power of networking in a job search. To network is to reach out to your family, friends, teachers, and other acquaintances. Let them know you're looking for a job, and ask them to tell you if they hear of any job opportunities.

HOW TO APPLY

The nuts and bolts of applying for a job will depend on the employer. At some workplaces, you can fill out an application right on the spot. The application might be a paper form or an electronic form, which you fill out at a computer terminal.

The application will usually ask you to list your name and contact information, your work experience (including contact information for previous employers), schools you've attended, hours you're available for work, and

Application fo

Position You Are Applying For

Date Available for Work:

PERSONAL INFORMATION

Last Name

Address

Cell Phone:

references—or names of people who will recommend you as a good worker. When you go to fill out an application at a store or other business, make sure to have all this information at your fingertips. If you're filling out a paper application, make sure you use neat, easy-to-read writing and fill out the form thoroughly.

THE RÉSUMÉ

Many businesses want applicants to submit résumés instead of filling out applications. A résumé lists the same basic information you would include on a job application—only you prepare the résumé yourself, ahead of time, rather than filling in blanks on a form.

Most people create their own résumés using word processing software and home computer printers, but you can also have a résumé made and printed at an office supply store or a copy shop. This option will cost more than making your own résumé.

Some employers want applicants to send in résumés by U.S. mail. Other employers want résumés to come in as e-mail attachments. The job listing will tell you what the employer wants.

All résumés should include the following key sections:

- Heading: At the top of the résumé, list your name and contact information, including your phone number, mailing address, and e-mail address. Don't use an e-mail address that includes a silly nickname or a joke (such as goofball@internet.com). For your job search, you might want to sign up for a new e-mail account with Gmail or Hotmail. Choose a professional-sounding address, such as TJones@gmail.com.
- Objective: This is a one-sentence statement of your job goal. Your objective might be as simple as, "To obtain an after-school job." Or your objective might be something more specific, such as, "To work with children at a summer camp."

A SAMPLE RESUME

Clara Yanez
111 Main Street
Detroit, MI 48210
313-555-5555
clara@internet.com

Objective: To obtain a position in retail sales where I can use my customer service and sales experience

Summary of Skills:
- Excellent customer service skills
- Sales experience
- Ability to work under pressure

Experience:
Lead Salesperson, school soccer team fund-raiser, fall 2010
- Helped organize annual candy fund-raiser
- Helped team exceed sales goals

Neighborhood Babysitter, 2008 to present
- Regularly babysit for five families
- Recognized by several parents for excellent dedication to the job
- Received several referrals

Education:
Franklin High School, Detroit, MI
- Junior varsity girls' soccer
- Honor Roll, Fall 2011
- Graduation date: June 2013

References available upon request.

- **Summary of Skills:** Here you can highlight any special skills you have. You might have gained them at another job, at school, or as a volunteer. Think about times you have helped organize something, such as a school dance; times you have taken a leadership role (on a sports team, for instance); or ways you have shown you can handle responsibility (for instance, taking care of younger siblings).
- **Experience:** If you've held other paid jobs, list them here. You can include short notes about your responsibilities and accomplishments on the job. Also be sure to include the dates you held the jobs. If you haven't held a paid job before, list any club or school activities where you've taken a leadership role.
- **Education:** List the name of your school and any special awards or honors you have earned there.

Once you have created your résumé, *ask somebody to proofread it.* You don't want to be embarrassed by typos or other mistakes. When employers are sifting through a tall stack of résumés to find the best job candidates, they might automatically eliminate the résumés with typos.

THE COVER LETTER

Whether you send it by snail mail or e-mail, it's a good idea to include a cover letter with your résumé. Your letter can be short and to the point, but mainly it should show a future boss that you know how to present yourself professionally in writing.

In the first paragraph, state the job you're applying for and explain why you are interested in it. In the next one or two paragraphs, explain why you would be a good fit for this job. Be sure to mention any relevant skills or experience. This is a chance to tell the employer a little more about what you've listed on your résumé.

A SAMPLE COVER LETTER

Clara Yanez
111 Main Street
Detroit, MI 48210
313-555-5555
clara@internet.com

January 13, 2012

Hiring Manager
Rad Clothes for Teens
16755 Woodward Avenue
Detroit, MI 48201

Dear Hiring Manager:

I'm applying for a position as a sales assistant at Rad Clothes for Teens. I feel my experience in sales and my great customer service skills would be a great fit for this position.

I'm currently a junior on the honor roll at Franklin High School. This past fall I took the lead in organizing the candy sales fund-raiser for my junior varsity soccer team. I helped our team exceed our goals and was told by my adviser that I have excellent sales and organization skills. I sold candy at a booth during varsity games, and I also sold candy at a table I set up outside my local grocery store.

I have a history of job responsibility, since I have regularly babysat for several families in my neighborhood. Because of my consistent punctuality and preparedness, I have received several referrals from families I work with.

I am eager to apply my sales and customer service skills at Rad Clothing. You can reach me by phone at 313-555-5555 or by e-mail at clara@internet.com. Thank you for considering my application.

Sincerely,

Clara Yanez

Clara Yanez

In the last paragraph, tell the employer how he or she can contact you and thank the person for considering your application.

THE REFERENCE LIST

In job-search lingo, a reference is anyone who can vouch for your ability to be responsible on a job. The best references are former employers, teachers, coaches, church leaders, and club leaders. Before you include someone on your list, ask if he or she would be willing to provide a reference for you. Most adults will be happy to help out.

DON'T LET FACEBOOK COST YOU A JOB

Kids love posting pictures and messages on Facebook, but be aware that most employers do a quick Internet search of job applicants before hiring them. The employer is looking for any red flags, or negative information, that might show up online. The search often leads to the job applicant's Facebook or Myspace page. So before you apply for a job, do a quick review of your online profiles. Type your name and city into a search engine, and see what shows up. Remove anything you wouldn't want an employer to see, such as foul language or photos

You might need to list four or five references when you fill out a job application at a business. You'll need to give their job titles, organizations, and contact information. People typically don't include references on their résumés, but they usually have a separate list of references ready in case an employer asks to see it.

HOW TO ACE YOUR INTERVIEWS

After an employer reviews your résumé or application and if he or she is interested in hiring you, you might be asked to come in for an interview. This is your chance to show the employer that you'd be a great fit for a job. Follow these tips to impress your future boss:

ARRIVE ON TIME

Make sure you know how you will get to the interview and how long it will take you to get there. If it's a tricky trip, perhaps requiring you to change buses, do a practice run. If you need a ride, make sure the person who's taking you is reliable and will get you there on time. If you are driving yourself,

These students practice their job interview skills during school. Be sure to look the interviewer in the eye and to greet him or her with a strong handshake.

make sure you know where to park and whether you'll need to pay to park. Plan to arrive at the interview five to ten minutes early.

DRESS TO IMPRESS

No, you don't need to wear a suit and tie to apply for a job scooping ice cream. But you do need to look professional. Remember, you're there to show a future boss that you will take your job seriously. At a minimum, this means no ripped clothing, a tucked-in shirt, and no flashy jewelry or makeup. Also avoid extra-baggy clothes, too-tight clothes, shorts, tank tops, low-cut shirts, and flip-flops. At a job interview, it's generally better to be overdressed than underdressed.

USA TODAY Snapshots®

Where job candidates make the most mistakes in the application process

Interview	32%
Résumé	28%
Reference checks	10%
Interview follow-up	9%
Cover letter	8%

Source: Accountemps survey of 1,400 chief financial officers

By Jae Yang and Sam Ward, USA TODAY, 2010

When it comes to landing a job, first impressions are key. If you have a job interview, come prepared and act professionally.

BE PREPARED

At the interview, the employer will ask you questions about your experience, your interests, and your skills—so be ready to talk. He or she might also let you ask your own questions about the job, so it's smart to have some questions prepared ahead of time. Many job applicants prepare for an interview by doing research about the

JOB SEEKERS SHOW RATHER THAN TELL; WEBSITES SHOWCASE VIDEO RESUMES

By Jim Hopkins

Leveraging one of the Web's most popular new formats, job hunters and corporate recruiters are adding online video resumes to their arsenals. More start-ups make these high-tech resumes possible. WorkBlast near Phoenix, Arizona, and MyPersonalBroadcast in Atlanta just launched services. HireVue in Salt Lake City, Utah, lets candidates record themselves answering questions to get a regular interview. Job candidates turn the camera on themselves to talk about skills and education and show work they've done.

Videos better capture personalities of job hunters and companies looking for workers, says Allen Weiner, research director for media and tech at Gartner. "It's more than text. You can show a lot," he says.

Job seekers started adding video resumes to YouTube about a year ago. There are now as many as 4,000, including Allen Ulbricht's. The Atlanta resident created his to get a job last fall as a senior project manager at EarthLink.

Ulbricht, 30, wanted to show the hiring manager his Web 2.0 skills, such as creating online video, rather than just write about them in a regular resume. "Action speaks louder than words," he says.

company, its products, and its future plans. You can find much of this information online.

BE PROFESSIONAL

Don't worry, you don't have to act like a lawyer at a job interview, but you do need to be polite and outgoing and express enthusiasm for the job. Avoid mumbling, looking down when talking, saying negative

He also wanted to show he's a techie with a sense of humor. In the opening shot, he introduces himself as if he's confessing to a self-help group: "Hi, my name is Allen Ulbricht. And I am a job applicant."

YouTube's success has spawned dozens of rivals. Among them:

- WorkBlast lets job seekers create a free profile page where they upload videos, a regular resume, and their photo. They can then send a link to the page to as many e-mail contacts as they choose.
- MyPersonalBroadcast lets customers track who downloads and watches their video. The company is targeting a youthful market: 17 million college students seeking internships, summer jobs, and permanent employment every year.
- HireVue works with employers trying to save money on recruiting by screening job candidates through video interviews before deciding on a formal in-person interview. Co-founder Mark Newman says such remote video interviews save U.S. employers money on travel costs, especially in the tech industry, where job candidates often live overseas.

—*April 25, 2007*

things about past jobs or past employers, or acting interested only in how much the job pays.

FOLLOW UP!

After an interview, be sure to *send a follow-up thank-you note.* It doesn't need to be long. It can simply thank the interviewer for her or his time and restate your interest in the job.

3 KEEPING a Job

Your boss will probably keep an eye out for you when you start a job to make sure you are doing well and are a good fit for the position.

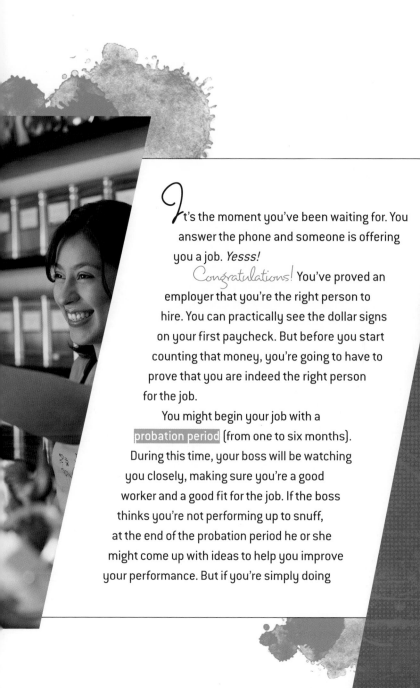

*I*t's the moment you've been waiting for. You answer the phone and someone is offering you a job. *Yesss!*

Congratulations! You've proved an employer that you're the right person to hire. You can practically see the dollar signs on your first paycheck. But before you start counting that money, you're going to have to prove that you are indeed the right person for the job.

You might begin your job with a probation period (from one to six months). During this time, your boss will be watching you closely, making sure you're a good worker and a good fit for the job. If the boss thinks you're not performing up to snuff, at the end of the probation period he or she might come up with ideas to help you improve your performance. But if you're simply doing

THE MINIMUM WAGE

U.S. law sets a certain hourly pay as the "minimum wage." That means that employers cannot pay below that amount, although they might pay more. Chances are, your first job will pay the minimum wage or slightly more. In 2011 that wage was $7.25 per hour.

There are exceptions to minimum wage laws, however. For instance, workers who get tips, such as servers in restaurants, can sometimes be paid less than the minimum wage. That's because their tips add to their pay, often bringing it above the minimum.

a bad job, the boss might even fire you at the end of the probation period. Don't let that happen to you. By taking some small steps at the beginning, you can pave the way for a smooth work experience for as long as you hold your job. Here's how to make it happen.

BE PREPARED FOR YOUR FIRST DAY

When you accept the job offer, make sure to ask what time to show up on the first day; what you should wear; and what, if anything, you should bring. If you don't have this information, call your employer ahead of time to double-check.

MAKE A
TRANSPORTATION PLAN

You might get lucky and land a job a short walk from home. If not, and you need to drive, bike, be driven, or take a bus or subway to work, you'll need to have a plan in place. And for every plan, you should have a backup plan as well.

If you need a parent to drop you off at work or pick you up, make sure he or she is available at the scheduled times. If you're planning to take the bus, check the bus schedule. Leave enough time to get from where the bus drops you off to your workplace *on time*. Also, make sure you have enough money for bus fare. If you need to borrow the family car, you're going to have to schedule that too, and check out your parking options ahead of time. If you're going to bike to work, scout out a bike rack near your workplace.

Make sure you leave for the bus early enough to get to your job on time.

DON'T BE LATE

Being on time for a job is pretty basic. Show up when you are supposed to show up—not half an hour later or five minutes later or even two minutes later. You might be surprised to hear that showing up late for work is one of the top complaints that employers mention about teen workers. On the other hand, being on time—or even early—is one of the easiest ways to make a good first impression.

If you are allowed to take breaks during your shift, make sure you return from them on time or early. Wear a watch on the job if you need help keeping track of time. If you're sick one day and can't go to work, call your supervisor as soon as possible, so he or she can find someone to cover your shift.

FOLLOW THE RULES

Different workplaces have different rules, and it's up to you to follow them. Some employers will give you an employee manual on your first day. If the manual is online, print it out. Read through it and highlight any rules or procedures that apply to you. Keep the manual in a convenient place at work so you can refer to it when you have questions. Some employers hold training sessions for new staff. Pay attention at these sessions and take notes if necessary.

On the job, always ask your supervisor if you're unsure about a rule or a policy. You can also check with coworkers.

DRESS APPROPRIATELY

Appropriate dress varies greatly from job to job. What's perfectly acceptable at one workplace might be completely out of line at another. Always ask your supervisor about any dress code—whether written or unwritten. Don't try to get around the rules—follow them.

Some companies want all their employees to wear the same color shirts or pants, and employees might need to buy this clothing themselves. You can probably buy what you need at a discount store for very little money. Other companies provide uniforms to employees.

No matter what the dress code is, always come to work clean and well groomed. Lay off the perfume, cologne, heavy makeup, and excessive jewelry. Always strive to look professional. Remember that you're representing yourself as well as the company.

This soccer referee wears a uniform of black shorts and a yellow-and-black regulation referee shirt. Each employer has its own rules about employee dress.

Your friends may come by the coffee shop where you work. Don't be distracted by them. You are there for work, not for fun.

ASK YOUR FRIENDS TO BACK OFF

When you're on the clock, you're supposed to be working and not socializing. So tell friends not to visit you at work. Of course, your friends won't drop in on you if you work in an office building. But they could stroll into a store, a coffeehouse, a restaurant, or other public place. If they do, don't let them distract you or get you in trouble with your boss. *Remember, you're there to work, not socialize.*

Don't take personal phone calls at work. Don't text, e-mail, or check your messages. Turn off your phone until you're done with your shift.

ACT PROFESSIONALLY

Behave professionally toward both customers and coworkers. Never use offensive language or curse words.

When you converse on the job, look the other person in the eye and speak clearly.

Never use alcohol or illegal drugs while working and never come to work under the influence of drugs or alcohol. Using illegal drugs could not only cost you your current job—it could also keep you from getting hired in the future. That's because a future employer might check with your old boss before hiring you. If the new employer hears about a history of drug use at your old job, you can kiss the new job good-bye. Many businesses even make job applicants take drug tests before hiring.

IS THE CUSTOMER *REALLY* ALWAYS RIGHT?

Maybe you've heard the saying, "The customer is always right." Like most sayings, it's partly true. Yes, customers are considered "right" because it's their money that keeps the company in business—and pays your wages. So if you work in a service job—for instance, at a store or a restaurant—you do need to treat customers with respect. This also means that sometimes you'll have to put up with people being less than polite to you.

But letting the customer be "right" doesn't mean you have to put up with abusive behavior. If a customer is angry, politely tell him or her that you'll need to get your boss. Then step away, explain the situation calmly to your supervisor and let that person handle it.

BE A TEAM PLAYER

USA TODAY Snapshots®

Teens' favorite entrepreneurs

Steve Jobs, Apple founder — **23%**

J.K. Rowling, author of the Harry Potter books — **17%**

Oprah Winfrey, media mogul — **14%**

Jay-Z, rapper and music industry executive — **13%**

Tony Hawk, skateboarding legend — **9%**

Source: Junior Achievement/ Sam's Club survey of 1,000 teens ages 12 to 17.

By Jae Yang and Alejandro Gonzalez, USA TODAY, 2010

Be willing to help out with projects when your coworkers ask you. This doesn't mean you should let yourself be taken advantage of, but always offer to help when you see that someone needs it. Stick with coworkers who have positive attitudes, and stay away from those with negative attitudes or those who gossip.

Many teens dream of starting their own businesses someday. They view Apple's Steve Jobs (who died in 2011) and other entrepreneurs (businesspersons) as role models.

KEEP A POSITIVE ATTITUDE

It's normal to have some bad experiences in the workplace. By keeping your attitude positive, you can grow instead of suffer from these experiences. For instance, if you make a mistake, don't try to deny it or cover it up. Nobody expects you to be perfect. Take responsibility for your mistakes, apologize, and move on. If you have a conflict with a coworker, bring it up with your supervisor rather than confronting the coworker yourself. If you're having personal problems, it's best to keep them out of the workplace. If you're having a family crisis that might disrupt your job, let your supervisor know.

FRESH SALMON FILLET 11.95

SCALLOPS 29.90

BEST COD FILLET 13.49

PALOURDE CLAMS 10.95

Your employer is counting on you to be honest, responsible, and positive.

WILD SEABASS

FRESH

4 MANAGING YOUR
Hard-Earned Cash

Open a New Account to Register to Win An Apple iPod

You can deposit your paycheck into your bank account or cash it at your bank.

*A*hh, payday. If you're like most working teens, this is probably your favorite day on the job. After all, you are working for a reason, aren't you? At most jobs, you'll get paid once every two weeks. Most often, every other Friday is payday. You'll usually get a two-part paycheck, with a perforation where the parts meet. One portion is the check itself. This is the part you'll take to a bank, where you'll either cash it (exchange it for cash) or deposit it into your bank account. If you don't have a bank account, you can take the check to the bank that issued it (the name will be printed on the check) and cash it there, as long as you bring a picture ID. You can also sign the back of the check and ask a parent or another trusted adult to cash it for you.

USA TODAY

Money

SECTION B

MONEY.USATODAY.COM

STUDENTS LEARN AS THEY EARN;
GETTING THAT FIRST PAYCHECK
MEANS FACING CHOICES, RESPONSIBILITIES

By Sandra Block

Summer is supposed to be a time to kick back and get a tan, but for many teenagers and college students, it's the busiest time of the year. Pinched by rising college costs, millions of students will spend the summer waiting tables, walking dogs, and answering phones.

Finding a job might be the easiest part. With a paycheck comes [many] choices and responsibilities. Some issues parents and students should discuss before the first paycheck arrives:

[No matter how little a child earns] there's a good chance she'll have some taxes withheld from her paycheck.

That's not necessarily bad, for two reasons. First, she can probably get most of the money back. Second, it will help prepare for a lifelong relationship with the IRS [Internal Revenue Service, the U.S. tax agency].

What everyone needs to know:

- A young worker will be required to fill out a W-4 [tax] form for every job he holds. The form includes a worksheet to figure out how many withholding allowances [used by employers to determine estimated taxes] to claim. Most teens and college students will want to claim one allowance on the form, says Brenda Schafer, tax specialist for H&R Block.

- Most employers calculate their withholding based on annual earnings, even if an employee works for just a few months. Many young workers can get most, if not all, taxes refunded by filing a tax return next year, Schafer says. "For most kids, when they've had just one or two jobs, it's a very easy tax return," she says.

- Tips are taxable. If a student spends the summer waiting tables, he needs to keep track of his tips and report them as income, Schafer says. That way, he doesn't have to rely on his employer's estimate of tips, which might be higher than the actual amount he received, Schafer says. If he must split tips with other workers, a log will ensure he isn't taxed on someone else's income.

—May 31, 2002

WHERE'D MY MONEY GO?

Before you run out to spend your paycheck, take a close look at the second portion of the check. This portion is called the pay stub. It lists your name, the dates you're being paid for (the pay period), an "earnings" section, and other information. The earnings section will show the number of hours you worked and the rate you got paid.

Suppose you worked ten hours at $7.50 per hour. You might naturally think that your paycheck would be for $75—10 multiplied by 7.5. *But you'd be wrong!* Why? One word: *deductions*. Deductions are amounts your employer takes out of your paycheck before you get your money.

WHAT DO YOU MEAN I HAVE TO PAY TAXES?

The largest deductions on paychecks are usually for taxes. U.S. law says that all workers must pay taxes on their income, or the money they earn. Yes, that means you. *Even teens have to pay taxes.* Tax money pays for things such as schools, roads, and other public goods and services.

To make it easier for workers to pay taxes, employers deduct tax money from workers' paychecks and send it directly to the government. At the end of each tax year, workers add up how

If you have a job, once a year you will need to fill out an income tax return form like this one.

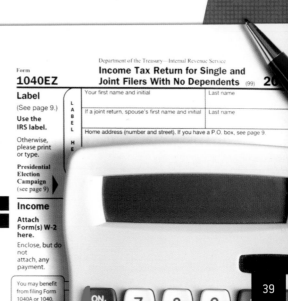

39

This teen reviews tax forms that he will need to fill out and submit to the government. You can usually pick up forms at public places such as libraries and post offices.

much they earned and how much tax money was taken from their paychecks. *Those who paid too much get a refund.* Those who paid too little have to send more money to the government.

Since most teens work only part-time, their yearly earnings are pretty small. This means they usually owe very little in income taxes—or no taxes at all. At the end of the year, most teen workers get a big tax refund.

Certain deductions are not refundable. In addition to income taxes, your pay stub will show deductions for several federal government programs. One is Social Security. This program

A TIP ON TIPS

You've spent the afternoon working at a coffee shop, and you're headed home with $11 in tips in your pocket. You had $14, but you treated yourself to a large mocha before you left. And now you're thinking a little snack sounds good. You stop at a fast-food place, and suddenly you're down to $6 in your pocket. Oh well, you'll still get your paycheck on Friday. But what if you had saved that $14 and the next day's tips and the next? After just four days, you'd have more than $50.

Earning tips at your job can feel like a big bonus every day. But it can also be a big temptation to spend too much of your earnings. Think of your tips as part of your pay. Set aside a certain amount to spend, and put the rest in the bank. Before you know it, you'll find your bank account growing fat.

gives money to retirees, people who are too sick to work, and other needy people. Another deduction will be for Medicare, which pays medical bills for retired Americans. Before you start grumbling about deductions, remember that Social Security and other programs are designed to help people who are too sick or old to work—and someday that might be you.

AVOID THE BUDGET BLUES

Now that you're making some money, you want to enjoy it, right? Yes—but make sure you don't enjoy it too much. If you don't pay attention, you might end up spending more than you earn.

You can keep on top of your finances by creating a budget as soon as you start working. This might sound tricky. After all, don't people use computers and sophisticated spreadsheets to make budgets?

Some people do, but all you really need is a small notebook. Follow this simple plan for creating a budget:

- Write down your monthly income. Include any pay you earn from your job, as well as other money you get as an allowance or a holiday gift.
- Write down your monthly expenses. Include any payments you make each month. This might include money for your cell phone, gas for your car, a bus pass, or lunch.
- Write down your savings goals for the month. What's that? You're not saving for anything? Bad idea. If you are earning money, you should be saving at least some of it for short-term and long-term goals. In the short term, you might save for new clothes or shoes. In the long term, you might save for college tuition.

Then do a simple equation: income minus expenses minus savings = your monthly spending money. Take that amount in cash and put it in your wallet. If possible, spend only that cash every month. Try not to dip into your savings or "borrow" from next month's paycheck. That's the quickest way to blow a budget.

USA TODAY Snapshots®

How kids pass the bucks

Types of accounts parents say their kids ages 13 to 22 have access to:

59% Savings account
41% Checking account
39% Debit card
35% Piggy bank
23% Credit card

Source: Echo Research for American Express and Jean Chatzky

By Anne R. Carey and Veronica Salazar, USA TODAY, 2010

When it comes to spending money, most American kids have lots of options, including checking accounts, debit cards, and credit cards. The trick is not to spend too much.

BE A THOUGHTFUL SPENDER

Sometimes a first paycheck can turn a teen into a reckless spender. Meet Joe Reckless Spender. He cashes his paycheck as soon as he gets it. He walks around with all his cash in his wallet. He buys whatever he feels like buying. Joe's feeling thirsty. There's a water fountain nearby, but Joe spends $2 on a bottled drink. Joe hears a song he likes. Sure, he could consider his budget and take a pass on the song. But instead, Joe opens an online account with a credit card and downloads whatever music he likes, whenever he feels like it. After all, he's got a paycheck coming in.

Joe's feeling good until the end of the month. Then he realizes he's bought two bottled drinks a day and spent $120 on beverages. Yikes. Then he gets his credit card bill, which includes almost $200 for downloaded music. Gulp. Add in the shoes he bought, that new video game, and a few other impulse (unplanned) purchases, and Joe has spent way more than his paycheck will cover.

When you get your paycheck, don't go out right away and spend it all at the mall. Instead, plan your purchases.

43

Don't be like Joe. Instead of being a reckless spender, you can be a thoughtful spender. The basic rule is to think before you spend. Ask yourself: "Do I really need or even really want this item?" Another good question: "If I spend this money now, will I feel good about it tomorrow or will I regret it?" A few more tips to help you become a thoughtful spender:

LOOK AT THE BIG PICTURE

You might tell yourself that spending $3 a day on a coffee is no big deal. After all, what else are you going to do with $3? Well, you could buy a car. A car? With $3? *Yes!* Just think about it: If you skipped that coffee every day, you'd save an extra $1,095 over the year. That would make a nice down payment on a used car.

OPEN A BANK ACCOUNT

Banks are the best place to stash your cash—for several reasons. First, banks will keep your money safe. Even if

Instead of spending your money on coffee every day, you could save it to buy a used car.

DIRECT DEPOSIT

Many employers use a direct deposit system to pay employees. Instead of handing you a paycheck to cash or deposit yourself, the employer deposits your pay into your bank account electronically. This saves you from having to go to the bank yourself. If you are paid via direct deposit, your employer will usually still hand you a paper pay stub, so you will have a record of your pay.

someone robs the bank, the U.S. government or an insurance company will pay your money back. Second, you can open a checking account at a bank. That means you can pay bills and make purchases by filling out checks instead of using cash. With a checking account, you can also get a debit card. Paying for things with a debit card is even easier than writing checks. You just swipe the card at a store or other business, and the money is automatically transferred from your bank account to the business's account.

Best of all, while your money is in the bank, it is actually growing. That means you can earn money just by doing nothing. How so? If you put your money in a bank account, the bank will pay you interest. Interest is money that borrowers pay to lenders. When you put money in a bank account, you are really loaning money to the bank. While your money is in the account, the bank can use it for its own moneymaking projects. For the privilege of using your money, the bank pays you interest.

5 TAKE Charge

Another job option is working for yourself. You could start a dog-walking or a babysitting business.

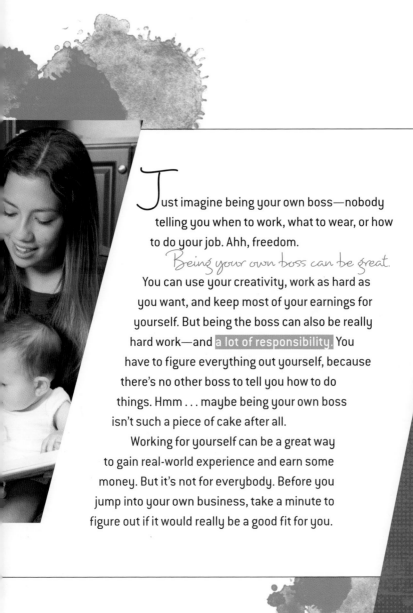

Just imagine being your own boss—nobody telling you when to work, what to wear, or how to do your job. Ahh, freedom. *Being your own boss can be great.* You can use your creativity, work as hard as you want, and keep most of your earnings for yourself. But being the boss can also be really hard work—and a lot of responsibility. You have to figure everything out yourself, because there's no other boss to tell you how to do things. Hmm . . . maybe being your own boss isn't such a piece of cake after all.

Working for yourself can be a great way to gain real-world experience and earn some money. But it's not for everybody. Before you jump into your own business, take a minute to figure out if it would really be a good fit for you.

CONSIDER THE PROS

Let's look at the positives of self-employment. You can set your own hours: you schedule your work for when you have time, not when a boss tells you to be on the job. You have independence: you decide how to run your business and how much to charge. You'll get lots of personal satisfaction when things go well. If you do a good job, your customers will praise you and perhaps recommend you to their friends. If you work hard and business is good, you might earn a lot of money.

AND THE CONS

But then consider the downsides. When you work for a company, you're guaranteed to get paid, even when business is slow. When you work for yourself, you won't have that guarantee. If business is bad, you won't get much money—and you might not get paid at all.

While you might not like your boss at the fast-food chain or the coffee shop, when you run your own business, you actually have even more bosses. Suppose you shovel the snow for

If you are your own boss, you will need to carefully track the money coming in and going out of your business.

five neighbors and three of them are demanding and unfriendly. Three grouchy bosses are worse than one. But if you want their business, you'll need to be polite, even when they're rude.

Finally, you have to keep good records when you run your own business. You'll need to keep careful track of your expenses and your income. And if you earn more than $400 a year, you'll even have to file an income tax return.

WHAT KIND OF BUSINESS CAN A TEEN START?

As a teenager, there are lots of businesses you're not qualified to run. For instance, just because you like animals doesn't mean you can open a veterinary clinic in your garage. You also can't get a real estate license or become a teenage lawyer or doctor. But lots of businesses are suited for teens. Here's a list of just a few:

- Babysitting
- Car washing
- Computer services
- Home cleaning or organizing
- Lawn care
- Party planning
- Pet sitting or walking
- Tutoring
- Snow shoveling

So what will it be? That depends on your likes and dislikes. If you're a natural caretaker, then babysitting or pet sitting would be a great business for you. If you love being outdoors, then lawn care might be an obvious choice. If you really like working alone, you might like shoveling snow for several hours a day. But if you prefer the company of others, you might

Teaching elderly people how to use computers is a good business for teens.

find that work unbearably dull. Likewise, if you crave peace and quiet, babysitting might not be the job for you.

HOW DO I GET STARTED?

First, research your competition. This may be as simple as taking a stroll around your neighborhood and reading the signs stapled to telephone poles or posted on bulletin boards. Are other people advertising their babysitting, pet walking, or snow shoveling services? Make a record of who the competition is, how much they charge, and how successful they seem to be.

After that, you'll need a marketing plan. This isn't as scary as it sounds. It just means figuring out how you're going to attract customers.

RESUME BUILDERS

Ordinary jobs are great ways to gain valuable work experience. But if you want experience in a specific career field, you might consider finding an internship or volunteering.

With an internship, a young person works for an employer for a short time, such as during the summer or for one semester. The employer serves as a mentor, or teacher, for the worker. Often interns are paid a low wage—although some internships are unpaid. Taking an internship is one of the best ways to explore a career field—and whether or not you like it. You'll also get practical job experience that you can list on your résumé. To find an internship, start by asking your school counselor. You can also search the Internet. Just enter "internship" and a career field, a company name, or your location into a search engine.

Another way to gain experience is to volunteer at a business or other organization. Volunteers do not get paid, but they often get to do interesting work and learn a lot about a career or an organization. Nonprofit organizations such as animal shelters, museums, churches, and senior living centers often need volunteers. Ask your school counselor for volunteer ideas, search the Internet or local newspapers, or contact a local organization directly to ask if it needs volunteers.

This teen volunteers at a ranch for disabled animals. Volunteering is a good way to get experience in which you are interested.

Putting signs on bulletin boards is one way to market your business.

Some marketing is free, such as telling all your friends and family about your business. Some marketing, such as placing an ad in a local paper, is going to cost money. Putting homemade signs on bulletin boards at the library or in local grocery stores won't cost you much at all.

Next, get your supplies together. This might cost you some money. For instance, you might need to buy a heavy-duty shovel for clearing snow or sponges and buckets for washing cars. If these start-up costs are more than $50, check with an adult to make sure your business plan is sound. You don't want to sink money into an expensive venture with no guarantee you'll succeed.

You might not be cutting the ribbon at the opening of a new store. But you should decide exactly when you're going to officially begin business—whether it's after your big school project is finished, once summer vacation starts, or after the first snowfall. Just make sure you start your marketing ahead of time, so you've got customers lined up when you're ready to start working.

SIT BACK AND LET THE PROFITS POUR IN

OK, just kidding about this one. In fact, your work is really just beginning once you launch your business. You'll need to make sure you're providing quality services to keep your customers happy, and you'll need to continue your marketing to attract new customers.

Remember also that not all the money you take in with your business will be pure profit. Meet Danielle, a young entrepreneur who runs a dog-grooming business. She charges $10 a wash, and in the first two weeks, she washes five dogs. A quick $50, right? Not so quick, actually. After expenses, she earns only $18 that first two weeks.

Here's how it happened. First, she needed some start-up equipment, including a dog brush and some shampoo. She covered those costs with a $20 loan from her dad. She also needed to attract some new clients. She made some advertising fliers on her home computer. But the office supplies, including fancy colored paper, set her back another $12. Between the fliers and paying back her dad, she was down to $18 in profits.

USA TODAY Snapshots®

Internship for experience

What is the greatest benefit for students or graduates in an internship program, aside from pay?

Top benefits:

Experiencing different work environments	31%
Improving soft skills such as presentation skills, etc.	24%
Acquiring technical skills	22%
Making industry contacts	12%

Source: Creative Group survey of 125 advertising executives and 125 senior marketing executives.

By Jae Yang and Alejandro Gonzalez, USA TODAY, 2009

You can gain valuable job experience through an internship. The skills you acquire might also give you an edge over other candidates when you apply for a permanent job.

USA TODAY
Money
SECTION B
MONEY.USATODAY.COM

DON'T HAVE A JOB FOR ME? I'LL MAKE MY OWN

More Teens, Stymied by a Tight Employment Market, Turn to Entrepreneurship

By Laura Petrecca

Eric has spent the last couple of months drumming up business. Faced with dismal employment prospects at traditional teen-friendly employers, the 18-year-old has turned his passion for percussion into a money-making venture. The Ohio high school senior set up a website promoting his services as a drum instructor, printed business cards, and spread the word that he was open for business. He has eight students, ranging in age from 8 to 50. He hopes to pull in more than $400 a month from lessons, as well as earn more money from performing.

Amid shrinking job opportunities (the unemployment rate for teens is higher than for adults), many of his peers also are embracing their inner industrialist. The Small Business Administration's Office of Advocacy doesn't break out statistics for teens and tweens, but says in 2006, there were 492,000 people younger than 25 who were self-employed. Figures for that year are the latest available.

But experts say this year's number will likely rise due to job scarcity. Already, the rough employment market has led kids to increasingly sign up for the entrepreneurial programs offered by youth-oriented groups such as Junior Achievement and the National Foundation for Teaching Entrepreneurship. "Kids are

But the investments in her business paid off. The fliers helped her land three new clients the following week, and those clients recommended her to their friends and neighbors. Soon her business was booming. Every once in a while, she had to buy more dog shampoo, but otherwise, she kept almost all her profits.

actively considering starting their own businesses," says Junior Achievement USA President Jack Kosakowski. "It might be out of necessity, since there aren't a lot of jobs out there. But they're also seeing parents and other adults that have been loyal to companies for years getting laid off, so these kids might be thinking, 'Hey, I might be better off being my own boss.'"

Many entrepreneurial kids will use their businesses to scrape together summer spending money, but the fledgling firms can blossom into something much bigger. As a teenager, Tommy Hilfiger sold customized clothes in his Elmira, New York, hometown. Microsoft [founder] Bill Gates co-founded a data business that focused on traffic counts, Traf-O-Data, when he was in high school.

Today, consider Leanna and Jasmine. As a grade-schooler, Leanna, 13, often was asked about what product she used in her long, dark hair. She soon began to sell that all-natural hair-conditioning pomade, which comes from a family recipe. She officially launched Leanna's Inc. from her family's home in New York in 2005. Business has gone so well, she's expanded her line of hair and body products to more than a dozen.

The impetus [motivation] for Jasmine, who also founded a body-care company, was an unpleasant experience. At age 11, her locks [hair] fell out after she used a chemical relaxer. Soon after, she was mixing up her own natural products. At age 13, with savings from her allowance and a $2,000 loan from her parents, she started her small business, now called Eden BodyWorks. Jasmine, now 17, says her company sells more than 20,000 units a month through a website alone. The products, which are produced at a facility in Harvey, Illinois, have also been sold at retailers such as Wal-Mart.

—*MAY 19, 2009*

If you're running a successful business, you should indeed be making some profit. Be thoughtful about how you decide to use that money. You might want to stash it in the bank and save it for college or a car. Or maybe you want to reinvest the profits to make your business better.

EPILOGUE
PLANNING *for the Future*

Working at a clothing store could give you experience for a future career in the fashion industry.

As a teenager, you might already have a career in mind, such as entertainment, business, or medicine. You might even be able to get a first job in your future career field. For instance, a job at a clothing store might be a good starting point for a future career as a fashion designer. On the other hand, your first job might have nothing at all to do with your career interests. But all jobs *offer you valuable experience*

Even if you don't have a future in lawn mowing, you can still learn important skills by doing that job.

in the world of work, and that experience will come in handy in any future career. In fact, most people end up switching careers several times throughout life, so it's hard to know as a teen where your career will take you.

But it's never too early to start thinking about your career future. Here are a few tips to help you along your career path.

Take Notes

On the job, taking notes doesn't mean writing everything down. It just means paying attention and noticing the good and not-so-good aspects of each job. For instance, do you like working for a big company or a small one? What's your favorite and least favorite part of your job? Is there another job at your workplace that you'd like to try one day? Gathering this information will help you pinpoint the kind of work you'd like to do in the future.

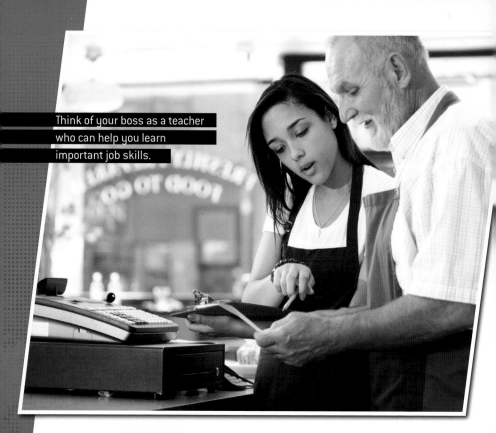

Think of your boss as a teacher who can help you learn important job skills.

Be a Learner

You probably feel as if you learn a lot in school, right? But you can learn valuable skills at a job that you might never have the opportunity to learn elsewhere. Take every chance you get to learn new software programs and new technical skills. Your boss will notice your enthusiasm, and you'll reap the rewards for the rest of your career.

Ask for References

When you're applying for jobs, there's no better reference than a former employer. So before you leave one job, always ask your boss if you can use her or him as a reference the next time you are job searching. Of course, do this only if you are leaving your job on good terms and you feel confident that your boss appreciated your work and will give you a good reference.

Don't Burn Your Bridges

It's all too easy to "burn bridges," or ruin relationships, at your job simply by becoming lazy when it's time to leave. People leave jobs for all kinds of reasons, so you shouldn't feel bad about resigning. Employers understand when teens need to leave jobs because of school or other commitments. But employers don't appreciate it when you don't give them enough advanced warning that you'll be leaving. Let your boss know at least two weeks before you need to leave a job—and work hard up through the very last day.

Always try to leave on good terms, even if you didn't really like the job. If you act professionally and work enthusiastically, your employer will probably give you a good reference, even if the job wasn't the best fit for you.

Don't Forget

Above all, remember that you're gaining more than a paycheck from any job you hold or business you run as a teen. You're getting a valuable chance to explore different career options and to test fields that interest you. As you plan your career path, make sure to remember what you liked—and didn't like—about each of your teen moneymaking experiences. You can use that information to land your dream job somewhere down the line.

GLOSSARY

APPLICATION: a form that a jobseeker fills out for a potential employer. Applications usually ask for the jobseeker's contact information, employment history, educational history, and references.

BUDGET: a financial plan that lists a person's income, expenses, and savings activities. Budgets help people track the money they have coming in and going out.

CAREER: a job field, such as medicine, business, or teaching, that a worker pursues over a long period of time

CHECK: a piece of paper one person gives to another, authorizing the payment of money from the giver's bank account

CHECKING ACCOUNT: a bank account that allows you to write checks to transfer money to other people

COVER LETTER: a letter that a jobseeker sends to a potential employer along with a résumé

DEBIT CARD: a plastic card that allows you to make purchases at stores and other businesses. When you pay with a debit card, the money electronically transfers from your bank account to the business's bank account.

DEDUCTION: an amount of money subtracted from a worker's paycheck. Taxes are some of the most common deductions taken from paychecks.

ENTREPRENEUR: someone who starts and runs his or her own business

INCOME: money you receive, whether from earnings, gifts, or other sources

INTEREST: money that a borrower pays to a lender for the privilege of borrowing money

INTERNSHIP: a short-term job that gives a worker experience in a certain career field. The employer serves as a teacher to the worker.

INTERVIEW: a meeting between an employer and a job applicant. Interviews help employers determine whether the applicant is suitable for a job.

MARKETING: the act of promoting a business or a product

MINIMUM WAGE: the lowest pay rate that an employer can offer according to law

NETWORKING: making personal connections that are beneficial in business. Job hunters network by telling friends, family, and acquaintances that they are looking for work.

PAY STUB: the portion of a paycheck that lists information on the worker's earnings, such as the pay period, the total amount earned, and any deductions

PROBATION: a period of several months during which a boss evaluates the performance of a new employee to make sure that he or she is a good fit for the job

PROFESSIONAL: conforming to a businesslike manner that is appropriate for the workplace

PROFIT: the money earned by a business after deducting the cost of supplies and other expenses

REFERENCE: a person who will recommend you as a responsible worker to a potential employer

RÉSUMÉ: a document that lists basic information about a potential employee, such as his or her skills, work experience, education, and interests

SELF-EMPLOYMENT: running one's own business

START-UP COSTS: the costs associated with starting a business, such as the cost of supplies

TAX: money that a citizen pays to the government. Tax money pays for roads, schools, armies, and other public works.

TIP: a voluntary payment made by a customer to a worker, such as a server in a restaurant. Many workers rely on tips to bring their pay above the minimum wage.

VOLUNTEER: someone who works for a business or an organization for no pay. Many young people volunteer to gain work experience.

LERNER

SOURCE

Expand learning beyond the printed book. Download free, complementary educational resources for this book from our website, www.lernerresource.com.

SELECTED BIBLIOGRAPHY

Barling, Julian, and E. Kevin Kelloway. *Young Workers: Varieties of Experience*. Washington, DC: American Psychological Association, 1999.

Brancato, Robin F. *Money: Getting It, Using It, and Avoiding the Traps*. Lanham, MD: Scarecrow Press, 2007.

Burleson, Kimberly Spink, and Robyn Collins. *Prepare to Be a Teen Millionaire*. Deerfield Beach, FL: Health Communications, 2008.

Deering, Kathryn. *Cash and Credit Information for Teens: Tips for a Successful Financial Life*. Detroit: Omnigraphics, 2005.

Ireland, Susan. *The Complete Idiot's Guide to Cool Jobs for Teens*. Indianapolis: Pearson Education, 2001.

ISeek Solutions. "Ready to Find a Job?" *iSeek.org*. 2009–2011. http://www.iseek.org/jobs/index.html (September 1, 2010).

State of Minnesota, "Explore Careers." CareerOneStop. 2011. http://careeronestop.org/ExploreCareers (September 1, 2010).

U.S. Department of Labor. Youth Rules! N.d. http://youthrules.dol.gov (September 1, 2010).

FURTHER INFORMATION

Bolles, Richard N., and Carol Christen. *What Color Is Your Parachute for Teens*. New York: Ten Speed Press, 2010.
This book will help young people figure out a career path to match their unique interests and skills.

Bureau of Labor Statistics: Occupational Outlook Handbook
http://www.bls.gov/OCO
Visit this website to find up-to-date information on hundreds of different types of jobs. The site includes jobs you can do as a teen as well as jobs you might want to explore in the future.

CareerBuilder
> http://www.careerbuilder.com
> One of the largest Internet job banks, this site offers thousands of job listings, including part-time jobs, as well as articles with career and job-searching advice.

CareerKey
> http://www.careerkey.org/
> This website has self-assessment tools to help you figure out your area of interest and learn about different types of careers. Also, visit the section just for high school students.

Coon, Nora E. *Teen Dream Jobs*. Hillsboro, OR: Beyond Words Publishing, 2003.
> This book, written by a first-year high school student, describes eleven different career fields that teens might be interested in, including film, fashion, arts, computers, and working with animals.

Donovan, Sandy. *Budgeting Smarts: How to Set Goals, Save Money, Spend Wisely, and More*. Minneapolis: Twenty-First Century Books, 2012. This teen-friendly book offers advice about how to manage your money. Articles from *USA TODAY* offer additional guidance.

Slomka, Beverly F. *Teens and the Job Game: Prepare Today—Win It Tomorrow*. Lincoln, NE: iUniverse, 2007.
> This book offers teens practical advice on how to choose a career, search for a job, and succeed in the workplace.

Snagajob
> http://www.snagajob.com
> Use this online job bank to find jobs that pay by the hour. Enter your zip code to get started searching jobs.

TeenVestor
> http://www.teenvestor.com
> Visit this website to find tips about starting your own business. The site includes business ideas and plans and real-life stories about teen entrepreneurs.

Wilkes, Donald, and Viola Hamilton-Wilkes. *Teen Guide Job Search: Ten Easy Steps to Your Future*. Lincoln, NE: iUniverse, 2007.
> Check out this guidebook for teens for information on finding a job and what to expect once you're working.

INDEX

ABOUT THE AUTHOR

Sandy Donovan has written several dozen books for kids and teens, including *Budgeting Smarts* and *Scheduling Smarts* for the USA Today Teen Wise Guides series. She has a bachelor's degree in journalism and a master's in public policy and has worked as a newspaper reporter, editor, policy analyst, and website developer. Donovan lives in Minneapolis, Minnesota, with her husband, two sons, and a black lab named Fred. She wrote this book because she's never met a person who regretted having job smarts—and because she hopes her two sons, Henry and Gus, will read it one day.